LET'S CELEBRATE AMERICA

MARTIN LUTHER KING, J
NATIONAL ME

A Stone of Hope

by Joanne Mattern

RED
CHAIR
·PRESS·

Let's Celebrate America is produced and published by Red Chair Press:

Red Chair Press LLC   PO Box 333   South Egremont, MA 01258-0333

www.redchairpress.com

About the Author

Joanne Mattern is a former editor and the author of nearly 350 books for children and teens. She began writing when she was a little girl and just never stopped! Joanne loves nonfiction because she enjoys bringing history and science topics to life and showing young readers that nonfiction is full of compelling stories! Joanne lives in New York State with her husband, four children, and several pets.

Publisher's Cataloging-In-Publication Data

Names: Mattern, Joanne, 1963–

Title: Martin Luther King, Jr. National Memorial : a stone of hope / by Joanne Mattern.

Description: South Egremont, MA : Red Chair Press, [2017] | Series: Let's celebrate America | Interest age level: 008-012. | Includes a glossary and references for additional reading. | "Core content classroom."--Cover. | Includes bibliographical references and index. | Summary: "History recognizes the leadership and voice Dr. Martin Luther King, Jr. brought to the civil rights movement in 1960s America. A 30-foot tall statue of Dr. King gazes into the future full of hope for all humanity. His words of peace are carved in the walls of the monument as a reminder to all Americans of the power of peaceful protest. Learn all about the first national memorial to an African American."--Provided by publisher.

Identifiers: LCCN 2016955009 | ISBN 978-1-63440-227-9 (library hardcover) | ISBN 978-1-63440-237-8 (paperback) | ISBN 978-1-63440-247-7 (ebook)

Subjects: LCSH: Martin Luther King, Jr., Memorial (Washington, D.C.)--Juvenile literature. | King, Martin Luther, Jr., 1929-1968--Statues--Juvenile literature. | Civil rights movements--United States--History--20th century--Juvenile literature. | CYAC: King, Martin Luther, Jr., 1929-1968--Statues. | Civil rights movements--United States--History--20th century.

Classification: LCC F195 .M38 2017 (print) | LCC F195 (ebook) | DDC 975.3--dc23

Photo credits: p. 11: Dreamstime; p. 13, 21, 22, 25: Getty Images; p. 23, 24: Imgimage; cover, p. 1, 6, 7, 8 9, 10, 11, 12, 13, 18: Library of Congress; p. 20, 25, 26, 28, back cover: National Park Service; p. 3, 4, 5, 14, 15, 16, 17, 19, 23, 27, 29: Shutterstock

Printed in the United States of America
0517 1P WRZF17

Table of Contents

Walking on the Mall

One of the most popular places to visit in Washington, D.C. is the National Mall. This huge park includes many museums and **monuments** to great Americans. Some of the monuments on the National Mall honor presidents of the United States. Visitors to the National Mall can find monuments for George Washington, Abraham Lincoln, Thomas Jefferson, and Franklin D. Roosevelt. Other monuments honor groups, such as Vietnam War **veterans**.

One of the most interesting monuments on the National Mall honors Dr. Martin Luther King, Jr. This **memorial** is for remembering the most famous **civil rights** leader in American history.

Aerial view of the National Mall

The National Mall

Who Was Martin Luther King, Jr.?

Martin Luther King, Jr. was born in Atlanta, Georgia, on January 15, 1929. His father was a **minister**. King was a great student. He skipped two grades in high school and was only 15 years old when he entered Morehouse College in Atlanta. After he graduated, he went to another school to become a minister, just like his father.

In 1954, Dr. King was put in charge of a church in Montgomery, Alabama. At that time, Montgomery, like all cities in the U.S. South, was **segregated**. Black African Americans and whites were separated in public places, including schools, buses, hotels, and restaurants.

Top: Martin Luther King, Jr. with his wife, Coretta Scott King, in 1964

Bottom: King's childhood home in Atlanta, Georgia

Dexter Avenue King Memorial Baptist Church
in Montgomery, Alabama

Boycott!

CONGRESS OF RACIAL EQUALITY

Many Americans participated in equal rights demonstrations. Attorney General Robert F. Kennedy addresses the crowd at a demonstration in Washington, D.C.

On December 1, 1955, an African American woman named Rosa Parks refused to give up her seat on a public bus to a white man. Parks was arrested. The African American community decided to protest. They staged a **boycott** by refusing to ride the city buses. Martin Luther King, Jr., became a leader of the boycott. He encouraged African American people to walk to school and work. People also shared cars to get where they needed to go. The bus boycott was very hard. But people did whatever they could to make it work.

Dr. King and his friends also took their battle to court. Finally, more than a year later, Dr. King and his community won. Montgomery stopped segregating its public buses. This was an important victory in the battle for civil rights.

Rosa Parks

The boycott made Martin Luther King, Jr. one of the most famous civil rights leaders in the nation. He went on to lead many other demonstrations against segregation. Dr. King believed in peaceful protest. Even though he and many others were angry about the unfair treatment they received, Dr. King encouraged everyone to work peacefully to change the laws.

African American demonstrators outside the White House

King, speaking during anti-war demonstration in New York City

Dr. King continued to speak out, even though he was arrested several times. He led marches against segregation. He also wrote books and letters. He told people not to lose faith. He told them they could change the world by being peaceful even when others tried to hurt them.

IT'S A FACT

In 1964, King won the Nobel Peace Prize.

"I Have a Dream"

Civil Rights March in Washington, D.C., August 28, 1963

On August 28, 1963, Martin Luther King, Jr. led the March on Washington. More than 200,000 people gathered in front of the Lincoln Memorial. Dr. King spoke to them. He said, "I have a dream that my four children will one day live in a nation where they will not be judged by the color of their skin but by the content of their character."

Slowly, segregation laws began to change. However, many people hated Dr. King and his message. His home was bombed and he was arrested several times. Then, on April 4, 1968, a man named James Earl Ray **assassinated** Dr. King while he stood on a hotel room balcony in Memphis, Tennessee.

Top: King delivering his famous "I Have a Dream" speech at the Civil Rights March on Washington

Below: Demonstrators at the Civil Rights March

13

Honoring Dr. King

After his death, people found many ways to honor Martin Luther King, Jr. Schools and public buildings were named after him. In 1986, Martin Luther King, Jr. Day was first celebrated on the third Monday in January. At first, only a few states agreed to celebrate Martin Luther King, Jr. Day. Now it is a national holiday that is celebrated every year by every state.

Martin Luther King Jr. Park in Oberlin, Ohio

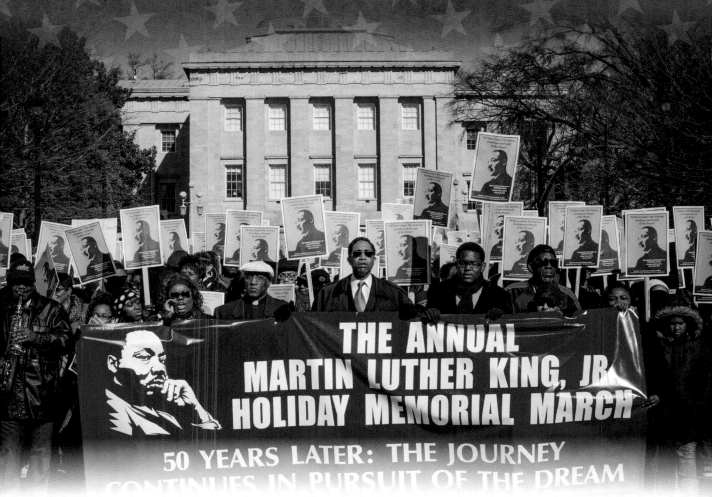

Thousands of people marched in Raleigh, North Carolina in 2014 to celebrate Dr. King's birthday.

People also wanted to build a memorial to Dr. King on the National Mall in Washington, D.C. When he was in college, Dr. King belonged to a group called Alpha Phi Alpha. In 1984, Alpha Phi Alpha decided to create a memorial to him. In 1996, Congress agreed. The memorial would be located along a body of water called the Tidal Basin.

IT'S A FACT

Martin Luther King, Jr. Day is celebrated on the third Monday in January because that day is close to Dr. King's birthday, January 15.

Choosing a Design

The new memorial would have to fit in with the many other important monuments and memorials on the National Mall. Show here: the Thomas Jefferson Memorial.

The Martin Luther King, Jr. National Memorial Project Foundation formed. The group held a **design** contest to create a monument to honor Dr. King. The Foundation gave each entrant lots of pictures and information about Dr. King. They also explained what kind of memorial they wanted and where the monument would be located. Each person or group who entered the contest had to submit three large boards to show his or her design.

More than 900 people entered the design competition. After three days, the judges picked their 23 favorite designs. The judges could not decide which one was the best. So they asked each person to submit one more board showing the design in more detail.

The first memorial honoring an African American, and especially a leader of civil rights, would need to be an impressive and powerful symbol for generations to come.

Thousands of people still find inspiration from Lincoln.

IN THIS TEMPLE
AS IN THE HEARTS OF THE PEOPLE
FOR WHOM HE SAVED THE UNION
THE MEMORY OF ABRAHAM LINCOLN
IS ENSHRINED FOREVER

The Promissory Note

When the architects of our republic
wrote the magnificent words of the
Constitution and the
Declaration of Independence,
they were signing a promissory note
to which every American was to fall heir.
This note was the promise that all men,
yes, black men as well as white men,
would be guaranteed the "unalienable Rights
of Life, Liberty, and the pursuit of Happiness."

28 August 1963
Washington D.C.

The ROMA Design Group won the contest. Its design showed a stone with Dr. King in front of a mountain. This theme came from a line in his "I Have a Dream" speech. Dr. King said, "With this faith, we will be able to hew out of the mountain of **despair** a stone of hope."

Next the Foundation needed to find a **sculptor** to bring ROMA's idea to life. Some of the members went to St. Paul, Minnesota. There they met a group of sculptors from all over the world who had come to the city to create public art. Several of the artists recommended a Chinese artist named Lei Yixin. After they talked to Yixin, the Foundation knew they had found their sculptor.

IT'S A FACT

King's quote, "Out of the mountain of despair, a stone of hope" is carved on the monument.

OUT OF THE MOUNTAIN OF DESPAIR,
A STONE OF HOPE

Left: Design development drawing of the memorial by ROMA Design Group

Creating the Monument

Lei Yixin got right to work. He filled his **studio** with hundreds of photographs of Dr. King. He also talked to King's family. Finally, Yixin felt like he understood who Dr. King was. He started to **carve**.

The sculpture's 159 blocks were carefully disassembled, shipped, and reassembled on-site.

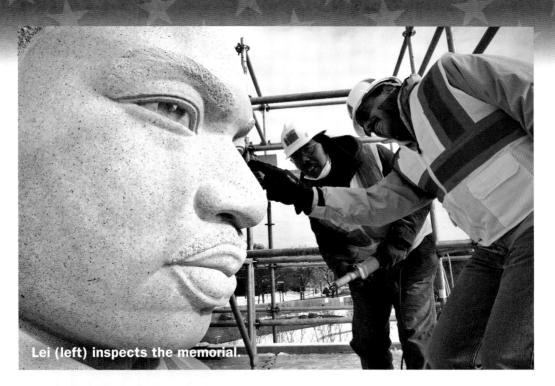
Lei (left) inspects the memorial.

First, Lei created a three-foot scale model of the sculpture. He used that model to build the actual monument. Lei carved the monument out of 159 blocks of pink **granite** in his studio in Changsha, China. Lei's sculpture shows Martin Luther King, Jr. stepping out from the mountain behind him.

When the monument was almost done, Lei took it apart. He shipped all of the blocks to Baltimore, Maryland. From there, the blocks were moved to the site of the monument in Washington, D.C. and put back together like a giant puzzle. Lei traveled to Washington to finish carving the monument on site.

IT'S A FACT

It took Lei more than 3-1/2 years to create the monument.

Important Words

Lei's sculpture was just one part of the monument. Once the blocks were put together, a stone carver named Nick Benson got to work. Benson and his team came from Rhode Island. They carefully carved some of Dr. King's famous quotes on the monument.

Nick Benson next to his work

DARKNESS CANNOT DRIVE OUT DARKNESS, ONLY LIGHT CAN DO THAT.
HATE CANNOT DRIVE OUT HATE, ONLY LOVE CAN DO THAT.

1963

One of the quotes carved on the monument caused some trouble. The quote was, "I was a drum major for justice, peace, and righteousness." Critics said that the quote made Dr. King sound like he was showing off and praising himself. In fact, Dr. King really said, "If you want to say that I was a drum major, say that I was a drum major for justice." Later, in 2012, the mistaken quote would be removed from the monument.

The Dedication

Finally, in August 2011, the Martin Luther King, Jr. Memorial was finished. Officials scheduled the **dedication** for August 28, 2011. Forty-eight years earlier on that day, King had given his famous "I Have a Dream" speech. President Barack Obama, the first African American president of the United States, planned to speak at the dedication.

Lei Yixin standing in front of the finished monument at the dedication ceremony.

Keep Pushing

At the dedication, President Obama spoke of Dr. King's patience and hard work. He asked Americans to remember his example as they faced difficult times. He said, "We can't be discouraged by what is. We've got to keep pushing for what ought to be, the America we ought to leave to our children, mindful that the hardships we face are nothing compared to those Dr. King and his fellow marchers faced 50 years ago, and that if we maintain our faith, in ourselves and in the possibilities of this nation, there is no challenge we cannot **surmount**."

President Obama speaking at the dedication ceremony.

However, Mother Nature had other ideas. Three days before the dedication, Hurricane Irene took aim at the East Coast of the United States. Officials did not want to have the dedication ceremony in the middle of a bad storm. They postponed the dedication until October.

A Memorial with Many Parts

The Martin Luther King, Jr. Memorial is located between the Lincoln Memorial and the Jefferson Memorial. The location was chosen to show a link between the freedoms all three men fought for.

The Memorial has several different parts. The Stone of Hope contains the sculpture of Dr. King. The site also includes a 450-foot long wall made of granite. Fourteen of Dr. King's most important quotes are carved into the wall. These quotes were chosen to show the important principles King believed in. These principles are justice, democracy, hope, and love.

IT'S A FACT

The Memorial's street address is 1964 Independence Avenue SW. The street number honors the Civil Rights Act of 1964, a law which gave rights to people of all races.

The finished memorial

Dr. King's words of peace are now preserved in stone for all to see.

Many cherry blossom trees flower around the Martin Luther King, Jr. Memorial. These trees were a gift of peace from Japan many years ago. These cherry trees bloom around April 4, the day Dr. King was assassinated.

The Martin Luther King, Jr. Memorial is only the fourth memorial in Washington, D.C. to honor someone who was not a U.S. President. It is also the first monument to honor an African American.

Visiting the Monument

The National Park Service is in charge of the Martin Luther King, Jr. Memorial. People can visit the statue any time, day or night. Visitors enter through the Mountains of Despair. They can read Dr. King's quotes and look at his sculpture as they walk from the Mountain of Despair to the Stone of Hope. At the end of the monument, visitors can look across the open plaza. The journey shows Dr. King's desire to move from despair to freedom.

The monument was designed to appeal to many different senses. Visitors can touch the granite and trace the carved quotes with their hands. They can see Dr. King's sculpture and also smell the beautiful cherry blossoms. They can hear the water in the Tidal Basin. All of these elements combine to give a sense of peace and hope.

"We can't be discouraged by what is. We've got to keep pushing for what ought to be, the America we ought to leave to our children..."

–*President Barack Obama at 2011 dedication ceremony*

Glossary

assassinated: murdered in public

boycott: to stop using a product or service as a form of protest

carve: to cut a hard material to produce a design

civil rights: the rights of all people to have freedom and equality

dedication: the act of honoring a place for a special purpose

design: a plan or drawing that shows what something will look like before it is built

despair: without hope

granite: a very hard type of rock that isn't affected by weather

memorial: something built to remind people of a person or event

minister: a person who performs religious duties

monument: a statue or building built to commemorate a historical person or event

sculptor: an artist who creates art out of stone, wood, or metal

segregated: separated

studio: the place where an artist works

surmount: overcome

veterans: people who have fought in a war

Learn More in the Library

Books

Jazynka, Kitson. *Martin Luther King, Jr.* National Geographic Children's Books, 2012.

King III, Martin Luther. *My Daddy, Dr. Martin Luther King, Jr.* HarperCollins, 2013.

Miller, Reagan. *Martin Luther King, Jr. Day.* Crabtree Publishing, 2009.

Pinkney, Andrea Davis. *Sit-In: How Four Friends Stood Up by Sitting Down.* Little Brown, 2010.

Web Sites

African American Odyssey: The Civil Rights Era
https://memory.loc.gov/ammem/aaohtml/exhibit/aopart9.html

National Park Service: Civil Rights in America
https://www.nps.gov/subjects/civilrights/index.htm

The ML King, Jr Research and Education Institute
https://kinginstitute.stanford.edu/king-kids

Index